SPORTS BIOGRAPHIES

FOR KIDS

PELÉ

1940
Born October 23rd, in Três Corações, State of Minas Gerais, Brazil.

1956
Signs his first contract with Santos at the age of 15, earning just $10 a month.

1958
At age 17, Pelé became the youngest ever winner of a World Cup (also Brazil's first win!).

> "SUCCESS IS NO ACCIDENT. IT IS HARD WORK, PERSEVERANCE, LEARNING, STUDYING, SACRIFICE, AND MOST OF ALL, LOVE OF WHAT YOU ARE DOING OR LEARNING TO DO."

Pelé grew up in a small village of São Paolo. His family was very poor. As a boy, he used to play with a sock stuffed with paper as he could not afford to buy a soccer to keep in his home. He even played soccer with mangoes during breaks.

As a result of the little money they had, Pelé had to take up various odd jobs as a child to earn extra money. He used to polish shoes or sweep floors at a tea shop.

His father had been a professional soccer player as well, but fractured his leg and never got to play again. However, he could teach his son everything he knew about the sport. Pelé later said that finding a mentor as young as he did changed his approach to soccer. He understood that learning was a major aspect of becoming great.

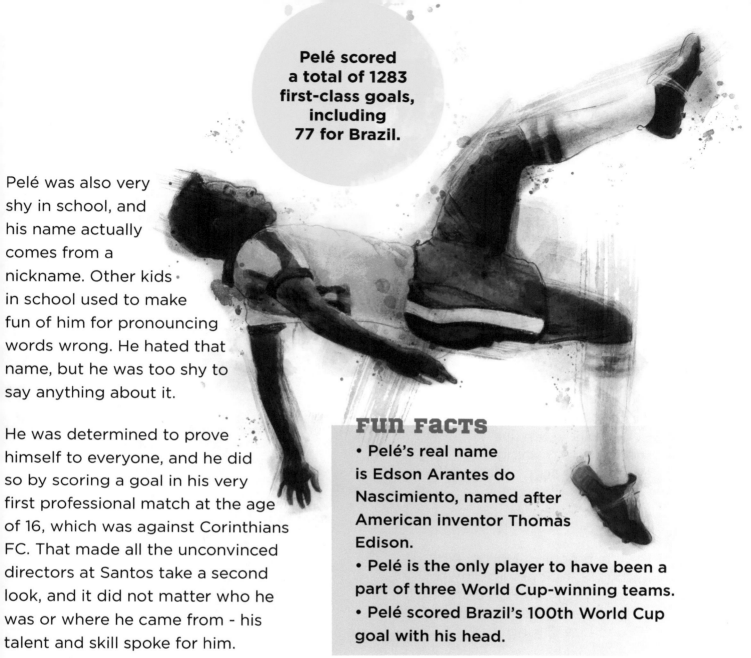

Pelé scored a total of 1283 first-class goals, including 77 for Brazil.

Pelé was also very shy in school, and his name actually comes from a nickname. Other kids in school used to make fun of him for pronouncing words wrong. He hated that name, but he was too shy to say anything about it.

He was determined to prove himself to everyone, and he did so by scoring a goal in his very first professional match at the age of 16, which was against Corinthians FC. That made all the unconvinced directors at Santos take a second look, and it did not matter who he was or where he came from - his talent and skill spoke for him.

FUN FACTS
• Pelé's real name is Edson Arantes do Nascimiento, named after American inventor Thomas Edison.
• Pelé is the only player to have been a part of three World Cup-winning teams.
• Pelé scored Brazil's 100th World Cup goal with his head.

AWARDS

| FIFA World Cup winning teams | Guinness World Records: most FIFA World Cup Wins & most goals scored | World Sports Award | North American Soccer League Championship | Athlete of the Century by the Olympic Committee | Brazil World Cup goal scored by him |

BRUCE LEE

1940
Born on November 27th, in San Francisco, USA to parents Hoi-Chuen and Grace Ho.

1954
Begins his extensive martial arts training and studies the art of Wing Chun, at the age of 13.

1959
Begins teaching Martial Arts in the US, teaching his own style called "Jun Fan Gung Fu", which literally translated as "Bruce Lee's Kung Fu."

FUN FACTS

• He was a cha-cha dancing champion at the age of 18.
• He practiced 5000 punches a day.

Bruce Lee's mindset was one word: LIMITLESS. He worked hard to convince himself that his body, capabilities, and goals had no LIMITS. He pushed his body and challenged himself to create new and unique moves in the world of martial arts, because he thought nothing was impossible, like a 1-inch punch that could knock a man back 16 feet (which he achieved!).

"IF YOU ALWAYS PUT LIMITS ON EVERYTHING YOU DO, PHYSICAL OR ANYTHING ELSE, IT WILL SPREAD INTO YOUR WORK AND INTO YOUR LIFE. THERE ARE NO LIMITS."

Being limitless and not feeling defined to one area in the world showed in Lee's career. He studied philosophy, psychology, and drama at the University of Washington. Though he was a martial artist and a teacher to many, he wanted to be an actor too. Lee chased all the dreams he had and didn't limit himself to achieving just one of his goals. He wanted to do it all, and ultimately achieved fame in Hong Kong and Hollywood for his success in the martial arts world.

Hong Kong Film Awards

Karate Championship

AWARDS

Guinness Book of World Records

Black Belt Magazine's Black Belt Hall of Fame

He worked his and others' minds into shattering self-made limits. He impacted the world of martial arts by breaking free from mental constraints and seeing it as an art combined with kinetics and physics, as opposed to traditional movements that don't work well in a real combat situation. He changed people's minds on race, as directors believed people were not ready or interested to see Asian stories told. He defied all those notions and inspired people around the world to break these constricting thoughts.

MUHAMMAD ALI

He fought one of his most famous bouts at 4 a.m.

1942
Born January 17th, in Louisville, Kentucky, USA.

1954
Police officer Joe trains young boxers and starts to train Ali at the age of 12.

1959
Wins the AAU light heavyweight title at the Golden Gloves Tournament of Champions.

The most powerful lesson to be learned from Ali was the power of intention. He felt he needed to have a vision of himself that destroyed all doubt. Before Ali had even won a fight, he declared himself "The Greatest." He infuriated professionals of the sport as much as he impressed them, because he held his hands unconventionally low, backed away from punches rather than bobbing and weaving out of danger, and appeared to lack true knockout power. The opponents he was beating at the time were a mixture of old people who were long past their prime and fighters who had never been more than mediocre. No one took him seriously, but he did not care about that. He continued to believe in his goal, practice, and work as if it was already true.
By 1964, he became the World Heavyweight Champion.

"I HATED EVERY MINUTE OF TRAINING, BUT I SAID, 'DON'T QUIT. SUFFER NOW AND LIVE THE REST OF YOUR LIFE AS A CHAMPION."

FUN FACTS

- His birth name was Cassius Clay.
- Ali was banned from boxing for three years.
- He starred in a Broadway musical that ran for one week while he was banned from the boxing world.

AWARDS

3

World Heavyweight Championships

2

National Golden Gloves Light Heavyweight Champion

5

Fighter of the Year (RECORD)

1

Olympic Gold Medal

He also defied all expectations of his place in society. He was born in the American South during segregation laws, within a poor family. That came along with prejudice and limitations, but he refused to be put in a box, and he actively fought and spoke against racism his whole life, even throwing his Gold Medal in the Ohio River as protest. He refused to join the army and go to the Vietnam War because he was a pacifist, and endured banning from the boxing world and a sentencing to prison over his principles.

Muhammad Ali understood that he could not be the Greatest without unbending values and principles he lived up to. Those included justice, hard work, and true self-belief.

BILLIE JEAN KING

She is close friends with Elton John, who wrote a hit song about her work.

1943
Born November 22nd, in California, USA.

1954
Aged 11, she moves on from softball to tennis and discovers her passion.

1961
Wins the Wimbledon doubles championship with Karen Hantz, the youngest team to win.

Billie Jean King rose to success during the 1960s in the USA, a very different time for women. She is one of the reasons that more women today have equal pay and are seen more as equals to their male counterparts. King experienced a lot of sexism during her time as a professional tennis player, a lot of moments where she was undermined, disrespected, and treated unfairly due to her sex. During one tennis tournament, Billie Jean was excluded from a group photo for wearing shorts instead of a dress. However, much like Ali, she knew that to be great you have to be incredibly strong physically and mentally, and those two cannot be separated.

"CHAMPIONS KEEP PLAYING UNTIL THEY GET IT RIGHT."

No matter the consequences, King fought for what she believed in, which was equal rights for men and women. She beat Bobby Riggs, former men's champion, in the famous "Battle of the Sexes" of 1973, and achieved equal prize money for men & women after threatening to boycott the 1973 US Open. To be great takes courage, conviction, and mental strength, which she constantly pushed herself to improve on by challenging herself to these uncomfortable situations. She was not born brave, she became it.

FUN FACTS

• In 1973, she became the first president of the Women's Tennis Association.
• She was the first woman to be named "Sportsperson of the Year" by Sports Illustrated.

That mental strength was placed in her physical skill as well. At the age of 13, she told her mom she had found her goal in life: to be the top tennis player in the whole world. She let that goal motivate her, because she knew that with enough hard work, she would be able to achieve it. She has said that she was lucky to be born with good coordination, but most importantly, she was obsessed. She practiced any chance she could, saving up her own money to buy a tennis racket, and spent more hours on the court than anyone else.

AWARDS

Grand Slams   **Singles**   **Doubles**   **Mixed doubles titles**   **Wins in 183 finals, in non-Grand Slam events**

39 — Grand Slams
12 — Singles
12 — Doubles
11 — Mixed doubles titles
129 — Wins in 183 finals, in non-Grand Slam events

MAGIC JOHNSON

1959
Born August 14th, in Michigan, USA.

1973
As a freshman in high school, he is named starter on the basketball team.

1977
Leads his team to Class A championship, named All-State for third time, and enters Michigan State University on a basketball scholarship.

1979
Drafted by the Los Angeles Lakers in the first round.

Earvin Johnson Jr. got his nickname "Magic" in high school, where he was well-known for his intense competitiveness, waking up at 7.30 a.m. to have more practice time than his teammates, and his creative and entertaining ball-passing and handling, which were like magic to the captivated audience.

FUN FACTS
• He was briefly head coach of the Lakers, before becoming a minority owner.
• He started a record label.
• He purchased 125 Starbucks stores.

"TALENT IS NEVER ENOUGH."

Magic learned about drive and creativity from his struggles with dyslexia. As a child, school was very hard for him. Dyslexia meant that he struggled with basic skills like reading and writing, and that left him feeling more stupid and less capable than his classmates, even though that wasn't the case. His classmates laughed at Johnson. Instead of thinking of himself in negative terms, and getting demotivated, he studied and worked hard. He failed, and understood that that did not define him. On the brink of failing the year, he went to summer school, and passed.

AWARDS

NCAA Championship

NBA Most Valuable Player

NBA Championships

NBA Finals Most Valuable Player

Grammy for Spoken Word

Olympic Gold Medal

His time as a basketball player and businessman were not short of challenges. Fear almost took over multiple times. On the court, the fears of battling the likes of Larry Bird, Isaiah Thomas, and rising stars like Michael Jordan were present in Johnson's mind. In the business world, Magic stated that his biggest challenge was to overcome his fear of starting his own business, and that it took him many years to start because of that fear of failing. However, he found ways of dealing with this.

He listened and learned from his competitors - Magic half-joked about how much he hated Larry Bird, who was his opponent in the Celtics-Lakers rivalry of the 80s, but he also said how much he learned from Bird, and how much of a better player Bird helped Magic become. He appreciated and valued every challenge he was faced with. He understood that failure was part of success, and trained twice as hard, knowing that his goal would be achieved.

CAL RIPKEN JR.

1960
Born August 24th, in Maryland, USA.

1977
Is drafted into the minors out of high school..

1961
Plays his first major league game on August 10th, scoring the winning run.

From a very early age, Cal Ripken Jr.'s whole life seemed to be baseball. His father, the coach and manager of the Baltimore Orioles, taught him about life through the game including the principles of hard work, being part of a team, and that you can improve your chance of success with practice, by working on your weaknesses as well as your strengths.

In 1985, Ripken sprained his ankle in the second game of the season, but finished the game and was back on the field for the next game. He severely twisted his right knee during a brawl with the Seattle Mariners in 1993, but still played the next day.

FUN FACTS

• Ripken is known as the Iron Man of his sport.
• His record-setting streak of 8,243 consecutive innings played still stands.
• Ripken was one of the founders of Athletes for Hope.

"I COMPETED AGAINST MYSELF TO IMPROVE. I WAS NEVER REALLY SATISFIED."

Right before the 1996 All-Star Game, a fellow baseball player slipped and broke Ripken's nose. He nonetheless played in that All-Star Game and again two days later. Injury or no injury, Cal Ripken showed up. "I didn't ever beg out," he said. "I just played."

Beginning in May 1982, Ripken played in 2,632 consecutive baseball games, a record many believe will never be beat!

American League Rookie of the Year

Gold Glove Awards

All-Star Game MVP Award

AWARDS

World Series Championship

American League's Most Valuable Player

Home Run Derby

Cal Ripken Jr. knew about pitching, hitting, and fielding, and he'd offer some of that knowledge to his teammates. But he knew that it's one thing to help people. It's another thing to tell them what to do. So he asked himself: "Where, when, and how do you help? You don't want to be critical or make someone feel bad. You maintain a rapport, do it in private, offer your experience and understanding of the game and make sure they know you're doing it for their benefit." He would then pick a time in the batting cage or the training room and say to them, "I know it's hard. Trust me, I know. But you've got to force yourself to do it right. Just put in the effort."

CARL LEWIS

By the time he graduated high school, he was ranked fifth in the world for the long jump.

1961
Born July 1st, in Birmingham, Alabama. USA.

1974
Coached by his father, who coached other athletes to elite status, he begins competing in the long run.

1979
After many colleges try to recruit Lewis, he chooses to enroll at the University of Houston.

Carl Lewis once said, "I always had the feeling that I was born to do something." That belief motivated him throughout his life. Even when his parents told him he was the third best-athlete out of their four children, and pushed him to pursue music instead, he had other plans. He went out into his backyard, measured off 29 feet, and stuck a strip of tape on the ground. The distance was one that even the world's best athletes could not meet, but Lewis began jumping toward it with singular determination.

At age 15, he suddenly underwent a traumatic growth spurt, shooting up 2 and a half inches in just a month, which forced him to walk on crutches until his body could adjust to the change. However, he persisted.

"CHANNEL YOUR ENERGY. FOCUS."

"Carl didn't just go after his goals, he stalked them," explained his father. "Carl set his mind on track and that was it. He said he wanted to be the best, period." Lewis began high school predicting that he would achieve a distance of 25ft in the long jump. Skinny and small, he lost far more meets than he won. "I believed setting goals was the only way I could get where I wanted to go," Lewis explained. "I studied track. Being around my parents and the club helped a lot. But I knew, in the end, it was up to me. I never lacked confidence. Even when I was younger, when I was losing a lot, I felt it was only a matter of time before I was the best."

AWARDS

65
consecutive long jump competition wins

10
World Championship medals

4
World Records

10
Olympic Medals

FUN FACTS
Carl Lewis was drafted by both the Chicago Bulls and the Dallas Cowboys but said no to both.

By 1984, Lewis became the first athlete since Jesse Owens to win four gold medals in track during the same Olympic Games.

NADIA COMĂNECI

1961
Born November 12th, in Onești, Romania, which was Western Moldavia.

1967
Begins gymnastics in kindergarten, age 6, and is chosen to attend an experimental gymnastics school.

1970
Begins competing as a member of her hometown team, and becomes the youngest gymnast ever to win the Romanian Nationals.

Her theme song is "Cotton's Dream" from the movie Bless the Beasts and Children.

FUN FACTS

- She became the first gymnast with a perfect 10 score in Olympics.
- She is the only athlete to receive the Olympic Order twice.
- She has a degree in Sports Education.

At age 14, Nadia Comăneci wowed the world with her flawless performances that left the judges incapable of giving her anything less than a perfect 10, a feat that had never been accomplished by any gymnast at the Olympics. She achieved this feat at such a young age not accidentally, but because of her self-discipline and hard work.

"HARD WORK HAS MADE IT EASY. THAT IS MY SECRET. THAT IS WHY I WIN."

Comăneci stated multiple times that she did not complain or shy away from hard work. When her coach asked her to do 5 sets, she would do 7, challenging and proving to herself that she could. She would train 6 or 7 hours a day, on top of school work. She knew that hard work was the only way to achieve her goal to become the best gymnast in the world.

She also knew that the only way to defeat any fear was to run straight towards it, because if she ran away, it would not disappear. It would simply appear somewhere else. She did not let fear tell her she was too young or too short, and she did not let the circumstances of her origin in a war-torn country make her believe she could not achieve her goals.

AWARDS

Olympic Orders
2

AP Female Athlete of the Year
1

Olympic Medals
9

World Championships
4

European Championships
12

World Cup Medals
3

MICHAEL JORDAN

1963
Born february 17th, in Brooklyn, Ney York City, USA.

1978
He starts playing basketball in high school, but he is too short to be on the team.

1982-83 & 1983-84
He is named NCAA College Player of the Year at the University of North Carolina.

When Michael Jordan arrived at the NBA at the age of 22, he and his team lost in the first round for 3 years in a row. Jordan understood that failure was a part of success, and used this to fuel his desire to learn and improve. The following year, he was chosen as MVP and Best Defensive Player as a guard. He would only win his first NBA championship in 1991, after more hard work and perseverance.

He was awarded the Presidential Medal of Freedom in 2016 by then President Barack Obama.

"NOBODY WILL EVER WORK AS HARD AS I WORK."

Jordan would train for hours after his teammates had left the court, and would use mental tricks to harden his motivation and mindset, like convince himself before a game that his opponents had trash talked him or had a fight with him, to rile himself up.
He proved time and again that success is earned by mental and physical training.

AWARDS

| **1** Rookie of The Year | **14** All-Star Game | **5** Season MVP | **6** NBA Championships | **10** NBA Scoring Leader | **2** Olympic Gold Medals |

In 1997, Michael Jordan got food poisoning right before a NBA Finals game. He slept terribly and had been throwing up left and right up until the big game. But, he proved that the mind is stronger than the body, because he convinced himself he had to play, no matter what, and that he could do it. They won the game, and Michael scored 38 points in 44 minutes, one of his greatest games.

FUN FACTS
• He has a phobia of water.
• He starred in the movie Space Jam.

DAN JANSEN

1965
Born June 17th, in West Allis, Wisconsin, USA.

1979
At age 14, he wins the national title on a skate championship.

1994
Wins his first Olympic Gold Medal, and sets a new world record in the 500-meter race.

At the 1994 World Sprint Championships, he became the first person ever to skate the 500-metre event in less than 36 seconds (35.76 sec).

Dan Jensen went to three Olympics in 1984, 1988, and 1992 as a favorite to win the 1000-meter race. However, every single time, he fell at the last minute. This earned him the terrible nickname "Heartbreak Kid," from the multiple disappointments of those races.

However, Dan wouldn't give up on his dream of winning a gold medal at the Olympics.

"I DO NOT TRY TO BE BETTER THAN ANYONE ELSE. I ONLY TRY TO BE BETTER THAN MYSELF."

During the 1988 Olympics, the prospect of winning was very bright for Dan. He had just won the World Spring Championship. Hours before competing, he was getting ready for his 500-meter race when he received a call. His sister, Jane, was dying of leukemia. She was only 27 years old. Despite this devastating news, Dan competed that day. He fell in the first turn.

AWARDS

First place, World Championships

Second place, World Championships

Gold Olympic Medal

Fun Facts
- He started skating when he was four years old.
- He is one of 9 children!

This failure didn't stop Dan from trying again, or losing his faith that he would achieve his goal, sooner or later. In 1992, Dan competed again at the Olympics. And yet again, he failed to win the Gold Medal.

The 1000-meter race was Jansen's enemy and biggest fear, but he soon realized that his feelings and thoughts towards that race were getting in his way, and he would not win with that mindset. He began to convince himself that he loved that race, that he could not wait to compete in it, and pictured himself as already having won it. That year, in 1994, he won the gold medal in the Olympics in the 1000-meter race. He learned that to truly succeed in his biggest challenge, he had to work on his mindset and point of view towards himself and towards that race, in order to vanquish it.

TIGER WOODS

1942
Born December 30th, in Cypress, California, USA.

1954
At only 2 years old, Tiger began learning golf from his father. Tiger shoots a 48 over 9 during his first television appearance.

1959
He won the Under Age 10 section of the Drive, Pitch, and Putt competition.

In order to win the World Championship 18 times, Tiger Woods had to overcome multiple obstacles and learn many things.

When he was 18, the doctors found two benign tumors. He had a lot of surgery, but over time continued to play golf. In 2003, Woods was in need of another surgery for his knee. Immediately after the surgery, he competed and won the Buick Invitational that very same year. Woods also experienced loss in his personal life. In 2006, his father died after a battle with cancer. He said, "My dad was my best friend and greatest role model, and I will miss him deeply."

"I SMILE AT OBSTACLES."

The Tiger Woods Foundation helps children worldwide with education and has reached 10 million children.

Over the course of his career, Tiger Woods has had 23 serious injuries, but after each one, he has made a comeback stronger than before. His rules for himself helped him continue his journey to become the best golf player he can be. Once he set a goal that would make him happy, he did not use his situations as excuses for not being able to do what he intended to do, because he knew that he was capable of anything. He proved it.

AWARDS

Masters Tournaments

Open Championships

PGA Championships

U.S. Opens

His desire to be the best allowed him to feel like the journey is never done, because you can always get better, and that's the exciting part for him. He also lives up to only his own expectations of himself, no one else's. Woods lives his life by his self-made rules. Be the best, he told himself, and then he defined what the best was.

FUN FACTS
- His mother Kultida is Thai and his father Earl was African-American.
- He is a Buddhist.

ALEX RODRIGUEZ

1975
Born July 27th, in Manhattan, New York City.

1992
Wins a high school National Championship.

1993
Signs with the Seattle Mariners after being selected in the first round of the amateur draft at the age of seventeen.

Alex Rodriguez has broken many records, including 500 home runs. This has put Alex's name at the top of leaders in home-run lists.

Alex was born to Dominican immigrant parents in Manhattan, New York. When he was four, his family moved back to the Dominican Republic and then to Miami, Florida. Alex began playing baseball when he was very young, learning the basics from his father, who was a baseball player back in the Dominican Republic.

During his childhood, Alex experienced loss when his father abandoned Alex, his mother, and Alex's two half siblings. Alex was only nine years old. With the sudden departure of his father, the family finances became very tight. His mother worked two jobs, one during the day and the other at night. Alex has often said, "My mother taught me the meaning of hard work and commitment." During this difficult time, baseball was his escape.

"ENJOY YOUR SWEAT, BECAUSE WITHOUT IT, YOU DON'T HAVE A CHANCE."

His teammates have attested that he is usually the first one practicing in the field and the last one to retire. When he is asked how he motivates himself, he says it's fear. Everyone feels fear, but he turns that emotion into fear of not knowing what giving it his all would be, and lets it fuel him to try harder.

FUN FACTS

- He is the youngest player ever to hit 500 home runs.
- Rodriguez became the first high school player to ever try out for the United States national baseball team.

AWARDS

American League Champion

World Series Champion

Major League Baseball MVP

All-Star Games

He is currently first in runs scored and total bases, second in extra base hits and RBI, and 4th in hits among all players in baseball history.

DOMINIQUE DAWES

1976
Born November 20th, in Silver Spring, Maryland, USA.

1985
At age 9, she won her first competition.

1989
At the age of 12, she traveled internationally to compete in Australia.

Dominique Dawes excelled in gymnastics from the age of six, and in 1996, she became one of seven girls to make it to the Olympics team, out of the millions who had trained and practiced. Dawes used what she learned from challenges in her life to make her stand out in her passion.

Dawes confronted a lot of criticism for her body not being what judges were used to seeing in gymnastics, because of the color of her skin, as well as her strong build. They said her knees were knobby and her legs were bowed. Dawes learned what criticism she should listen to, and to not pay attention to silly comments about her body made by people trying to make her fit into a mold she did not fit in.

"DON'T SET YOUR GOALS TO BE A STAR. SET YOUR GOALS TO BE THE BEST THAT YOU CAN BE AND GO FROM THERE."

She worked on her strengths and weaknesses. She combined gracefulness of the sport with her aggressive and ambitious personality to create her own unique form of performing, which many became fascinated by. She did not try to fit the mold. She learned to do it her way, as excellently as she could.

Fun Facts

• Dawes became the first African-American Olympic gymnast to win a medal in any individual gymnastics event.
• Dawes was best known for her back-to-back tumbling on the floor.

Later on, she did not just stop at gymnastics.
She attended Stanford University on an athletic scholarship, and pursued a degree in arts. She pursued acting, broadcasting, and in 2000, decided to dedicate her energy towards helping others. She is a major force in many organizations that empower kids to live healthy lives. Whatever she dedicates herself to, she puts her whole energy into it.

AWARDS

Olympics Gold Medal

Olympics Bronze Medals

World Championships Silver Medals

World Championships Silver Medals

MICHELLE KWAN

1980
Born July 7th, in California, USA.

1985
Learns to figure skate at the age of 5, following her siblings who skated and skied.

1988
Begins to train professionally and compete.

1994
Wins the World Junior Championships at age 14.

At the 1998 Olympics, Michelle Kwan was a favorite to win the Gold Medal for figure skating. She skated a flawless, mistake-free routine. Yet she came away with the Silver Medal that year because her teammate, Tara Lipinski, skated a once-in-a-lifetime performance that was even better. Unlike most Silver Medal winners who "lost the Gold," Kwan was genuinely happy.

In 1996, Michelle won both the US Championships and the World Championships.

She had controlled what she could, did her best, and came away satisfied and fulfilled. She embraced the internal reward of her personal accomplishment. And that's the ultimate key to feeling successful: focus on your own rewards, and your own best, instead of comparing your success to others.

"I DIDN'T LOSE THE GOLD. I WON THE SILVER."

Kwan focused on her strengths as well as her weaknesses, and soon learned to perfect her own version of the sport. She became known for clean, quiet and graceful skating performances, and she performed multiple skating moves to perfection, earning her the United States Olympic Committee's title "Athlete of the Month" fourteen times, which is more than any other athlete, male or female.

After competing in the Olympics twice, Kwan dedicated the passion and drive learned at sports towards her studies, and became a diplomat for the United States. She said the setbacks she experienced on the world stage at the Olympics only made her hardships during school more manageable. "That's the grit and perseverance that you learn in sports," Kwan said. "You fall every day, but you learn how to do it better next time. That's a life lesson."

AWARDS

Olympic Silver Medal

Olympic Bronze Medal

World Championships

US Championships

ZLATAN IBRAHIMOVIĆ

1981
Born October 3rd, in Malmö, Sweden.

1987
Begins playing soccer at the age of 6.

1996
Wins the Under Age 10 section of the Drive, Pitch, and Putt competition.

Before becoming one of the greatest strikers of all time, Zlatan Ibrahimović had a hard childhood that led to a lot of troubles in his life. His mother would hit him a lot, and his parents separated when he was very young. His father was not very present while he was a kid, which led to a lot of anger and frustration for Ibrahimović. He had days where he would go hungry, and even stole from shops. He was heading straight down a path of crime and violence.

FUN FACTS
• He's got two black belts in Taekwondo.
• There is a word in the Swedish Dictionary named after him: 'To Zlatan' means to dominate or do something with extreme talent!

"I DID MANY STUPID THINGS. I MADE MANY MISTAKES, BUT I LEARNT FROM EVERYTHING. I STILL MAKE MISTAKES; I STILL LEARN FROM THEM. "

He is Sweden's all-time goal-scorer!

5

Top Scorer

14

Soccerer of the Year

AWARDS

4

FIFA World Cups

3

UEFA Super Cups

However, he found something to dedicate all his time and focus to: soccer. "I wanted to stand up to the whole world and show everybody who'd doubted me who I really was," he said. The soccer pitch became his proving ground, with loud games extending long into the night. Just like the courts of Johnson or Jordan, winning wasn't enough. You had to play with style and panache. Tricks and moves were often more important than goals; that was how you got noticed.

As a boy, Ibrahimović was a massive fan of Ronaldo, and would study his games and movements, already learning from a young age how important practice and learning is to achieving your goals. Today, he uses his toughness in a positive way, showing confidence and strength during his matches, which intimidates his opponents. He found multiple ways to use his obstacles to his advantage, making him the champion we know today.

ROGER FEDERER

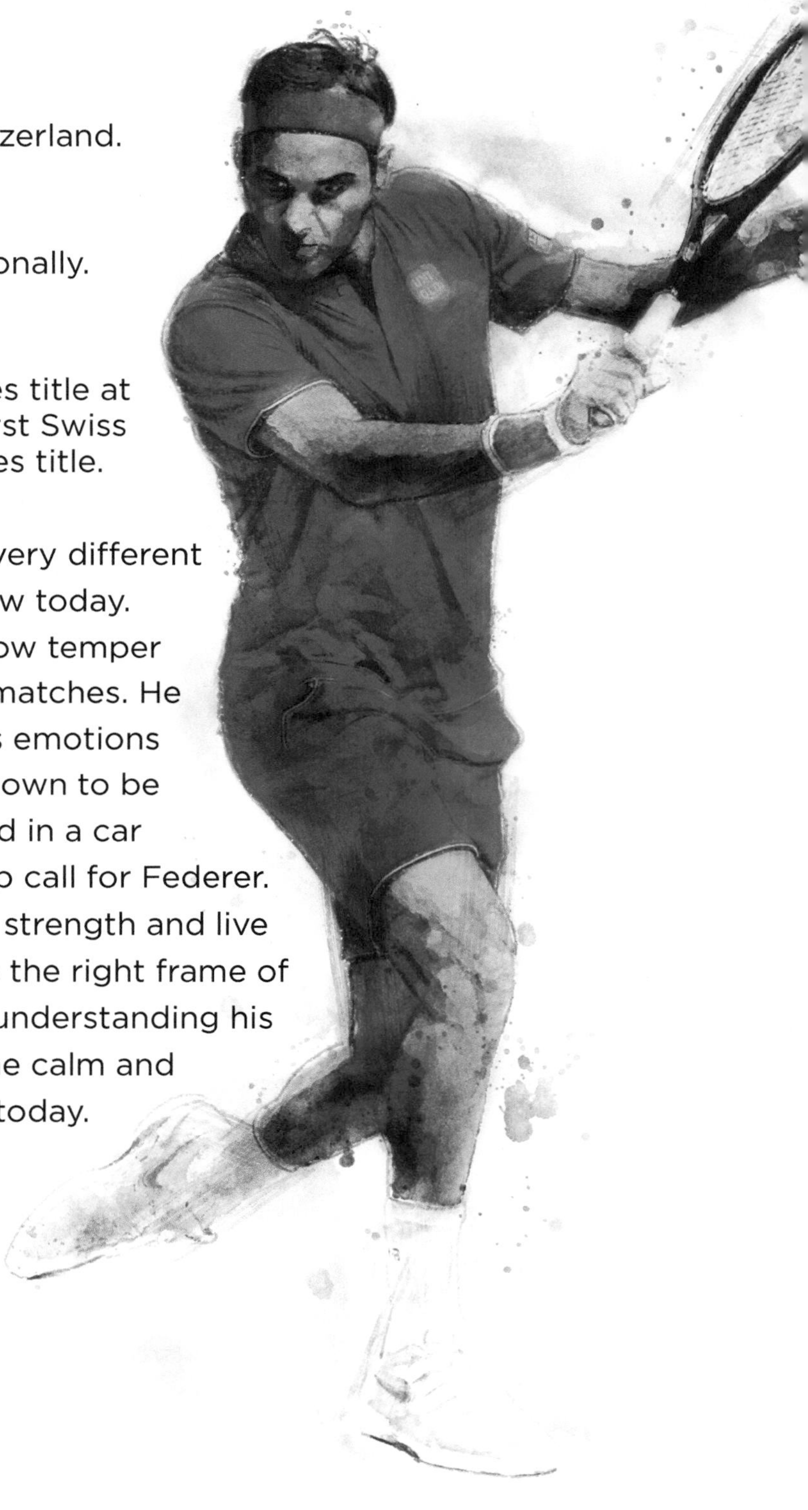

1981
Born August 8th, in Basel, Switzerland.

1998
Started playing tennis professionally.

2003
Won his first Grand Slam singles title at Wimbledon and became the first Swiss man to win a Grand Slam singles title.

In his early career, Federer was a very different tennis player than the one we know today. He would often break rackets, throw temper tantrums and take himself out of matches. He struggled a lot with controlling his emotions and concentration. He was also known to be quite lazy. But when his coach died in a car accident, it was a massive wake-up call for Federer. He decided to improve his mental strength and live up to his potential. By getting into the right frame of mind with a positive attitude and understanding his emotions, Federer matured into the calm and smooth champion he is known as today.

Roger Federer has been the world's No. 1 in the ATP rankings a total of 310 weeks - including a record of 237 consecutive weeks.

"BELIEVE IN THE LONG-TERM PLAN, BUT YOU NEED THE SHORT-TERM GOALS TO MOTIVATE AND INSPIRE YOU."

During the 2016 season, at nearly 35, he had to recover from a torn meniscus in his knee. Many doubted that he would be able to return. 6 months of patience and hard work showed results: Federer seized the 2017 Australian Open title. By learning to adapt, improve and advance, he's continued to stay atop a sport that isn't often kind to players in their 30s.

Grand Slam men's singles titles

ATP singles titles

AWARDS

Olympic Gold Medal

Olympic Silver Medal

Fun Facts

• One of his signature moves is called the "SABR" (Sneak Attack By Roger). It consists of moving up the court during the second serve of the opponent in an attempt to throw him off guard.
• He can speak six languages.

Federer turned himself into a positive thinker, and says: "I try to push myself not to get upset and stay positive, and that's what my biggest improvement is over all those years." That has helped him during difficult times, enabling him to "play with pain, play with problems, play in all sorts of conditions."

SERENA WILLIAMS

1981
Born September 26th, in Michigan, USA.

1985
Learns to play tennis from her parents at the age of 4.

1990
Her family moves so she can attend a tennis academy, and begins to play tournaments.

1991
Ranks first in the Junior United States Tennis Association.

Serena has a very famous older sister who is also a tennis player, named Venus Williams.

Serena Williams had to face a lot of obstacles to reach where she wanted to go. She began playing at the age of four, in Compton, Los Angeles, a very dangerous neighborhood at the time. She was at times risking her life to be able to train, but she did not use this as an excuse to not show up. She used this challenge to strengthen her abilities. She said: "If you can keep playing tennis when somebody is shooting a gun down the street, that's concentration."

People also doubted her a lot. When they met, her coach told her she was "just average" at tennis. She did not let anyone's opinions stop her in the motivation to become the best that she could be. Because of ignorance and prejudice, many in the audience booed the first times she played on the courts, as tennis was played mostly by white men, and she was a proud, black woman.

She defied all odds because she was passionate and determined to become the best tennis player in the world, and she had put in the work to back this up. When she won her first tournament, instead of cheering, people booed harder. But her family cheered for her, and she cried tears of joy that drowned out the ignorant people, because she knew that she was doing this to prove it to herself. Williams has said multiple times that part of overcoming obstacles and ultimately achieving success is ignoring the odds and what people think— believe in yourself.

"YOU HAVE TO BELIEVE IN YOURSELF WHEN NO ONE ELSE DOES."

AWARDS

23
Grand Slam Titles

4
Olympic Gold Medals

73
career titles

FUN FACTS

• Serena and her sister Venus were homeschooled by their father from elementary to high school to have more time to practice tennis.

• From 2000 to 2003 she attended fashion school at The Art Institute of Fort Lauderdale.

CRISTIANO RONALDO

"Blood, toil, and sweat" are the main principles of this Portuguese player.

1985
Born February 5th, in Funchal, Portugal.

1997
Is signed by Sporting CP at the age of 12.

2003
Is signed by Manchester United.

FUN FACTS

• At 15 years old, he had a heart surgery due to a rare heart condition that made his heart race too fast.
• His jump generates five times more power than that of a wild cheetah as it jumps in full flight.

Ronaldo was born in the small town of Funchal in Madeira, Portugal, into a very poor family. He used to roll old clothes into a ball to play soccer with it in the streets. His soccer teammates would make fun of him because his father cleaned the locker rooms to make extra money.

All of Ronaldo's frustration and sadness had no place to go, and one day, he even threw a chair at his teacher, which got him expelled from school. To deal with all these feelings, his parents encouraged him to put all his energy and drive into his sport.

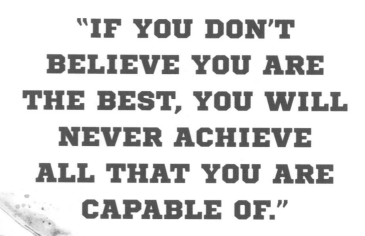

"IF YOU DON'T BELIEVE YOU ARE THE BEST, YOU WILL NEVER ACHIEVE ALL THAT YOU ARE CAPABLE OF."

He decided he wanted to become the best soccer player of all time. He trained extremely hard, from morning to evening. He found new ways to challenge himself, like using weights on each foot while dribbling with the ball to try and make himself faster. He spoke and listened to more experienced players.

He understood from the start that for sports, the mental is just as important as the physical. He convinced himself he was destined to be at the top. All that mattered to him was staying one step ahead of everyone, and becoming the greatest soccer player in history. That continues to drive him to this day, and he uses that mindset as a constant motivator.

AWARDS

2

Best FIFA Men's Player

5

Ballons d'Or

1

Player of the Year

4

FIFA World Cups

4

UEFA Best Player in Europe

ALLYSON FELIX

1985
Born November 18th, in California, USA.

1999
As a freshman in high school, she tries out for the track team, excelling from the start.

2004
Aged only 18, she competes in her first Olympics and finishes second in the 200-meter race.

Allyson Felix defied the idea that to be successful at your skill, you have to have started from a very young age. Felix began racing at the age of 15, and dedicated her entire focus and energy to running as soon as she discovered her passion.

For her, the key to success is having something that motivates her towards the finish line. For her, it is her family's happiness when she achieves her goal. Another source of motivation is her history, her past that fuels her towards the future. One key part of her past is the feeling of failure from her losses at two Olympics. She turned that sense of failure into something useful, by letting it useful, by letting it push her to never want to feel that way again. As Felix says, "I'm not afraid of losing. I lose much more than I win."

"ONE STEP AT A TIME, ONE DAY AT A TIME."

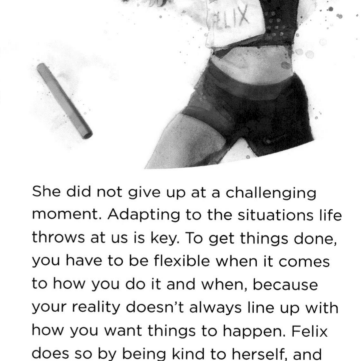

In the 2016 Olympics, during the 400m run in the USA team, Felix collided with another runner and dropped the baton mid-race. However, Felix demonstrated a key quality of leaders and winners: she re-focused and adapted to the situation. She noticed as the baton was falling and grabbed it, yelled to her teammate to continue to run and finish the race, and finish the race, and focus on the task at hand.

FUN FACTS

• She was the first athlete to win 2 IAAF Diamond League event trophies (200-meter and 400-meter) in the same year.
• She missed her senior prom to go to a track meet.

She did not give up at a challenging moment. Adapting to the situations life throws at us is key. To get things done, you have to be flexible when it comes to how you do it and when, because your reality doesn't always line up with how you want things to happen. Felix does so by being kind to herself, and being flexible with how and when she arrives at her goal.

AWARDS

7
Olympic Gold Medals

3
Olympic Silver Medals

1
Olympic Bronze Medal

18
18 World Championships

LIONEL MESSI

1987
Born July 24th, in Rosario, Argentina.

1997
Aged 10, he is diagnosed with a growth hormone deficiency.

2000
Joins FC Barcelona at age 13 and moves to Spain.

At age 10, Messi was diagnosed with a growth hormone deficiency. Soccer players come in all sizes, and smaller players are usually the faster and more skilled ones, but Messi was getting to a point where he was too small. There's not much you can do if your opponent has double your stride and can push you off the ball with ease. Even now, he is shorter than almost all of the pro players that he goes up against, described as the "little genius."

Because of his condition, he would have to have a medical treatment, but his club and his family could not afford to cover his medication.

"IT TOOK ME 17 YEARS AND 114 DAYS TO BECOME AN OVERNIGHT SUCCESS."

FUN FACTS
• He was nicknamed The Flea because of how small he was.
• His first contract to join FC Barcelona was signed on the back of a napkin.

Instead of giving up, he chose to use his lower center of gravity and focus his mind and energy on his greater agility, his greater balance, his greater speed, and his greater ball control. He practiced more and more every day, understanding how to use his disadvantage as a strength. By doing that, he was chosen by FC Barcelona at the young age of 13, who paid for his treatment.

He practiced more and more every day. He looked for help from figures who were mentors and friends, like Ronaldinho. Over time and with effort, he became the world-renowned legend he is today.

AWARDS

Olympic Gold Medal

Copa America

FIFA World Player

FIFA Ballon d'Or

European Golden Shoe

WHAT ARE THE GOALS THAT
YOU'VE SET FOR YOURSELF? HOW
DO YOU PLAN TO ACHIEVE THEM?

CPSIA information can be obtained
at www.ICGtesting.com
Printed in the USA
BVHW021532151122
651984BV00009B/606